Voices of the Earth

Scott Little Crow

Llumina Press

Copyright 2004 Scott Silverston

All rights reserved. No part of this publication may be reproduced or transmitted in any form or by any means electronic or mechanical, including photocopy, recording, or any information storage and retrieval system, without permission in writing from both the copyright owner and the publisher.

Requests for permission to make copies of any part of this work should be mailed to Permissions Department, Llumina Press, PO BOX 772246, CORAL SPRINGS, FL 33077-2246

ISBN: 1-932560-01-7
Printed in the United States of America

This book is dedicated to everyone who has supported me along the journey and to Spider, the weaver of the web.

About The Cover Painting

Pele, Hawaiian Goddess of the Volcano

Watercolor by Steve Davis (Esteban)

Dedicated to Raychelle

To learn more about Esteban's artwork go to
http: / / stevedavisartist.com

About The Author

Scott Silverston was born in New York City, graduated from Duke University (BA), California College of Ayurveda (CAS) and the National Outdoor Leadership School (Outdoor Educator).

He was given the name "Little Crow" by Carol Proudfoot-Edgar, a Lakota medicine woman. Like the rest of us, he is an imperfect human being doing the best he can.

If you would like to contact the author you may do so at

www.scottlittlecrow.com

Or via mail:

P.O. Box 1386
Kilauea, Hi 96754

About This Book

Sharing this work is something I have to do. Like playing music or making art, it is an act of creation, an unfolding of life itself and an affirmation of my purpose in this world.

<u>Voices of the Earth</u> is a collection of teachings from the web of life. The web is alive. It is alive not just with humans but also with the spirits of animals, trees, rocks and insects. It is alive with the vibrations of mountains, canyons, streams and oceans.

The teachings contained herein I received directly from the spirits with whom we share the Earth. I bring them to you exactly as they came to me; from the source, without interpretation or commentary, without dilution.

<u>Voices of the Earth</u> is a book about healing our separation. It is about reconnecting. It is a guidebook to help us open our ears, our hearts and our minds.

I encourage you to commune directly with spirit and to gather your own personal wisdom from the field of life. Go outside, talk to the plants and trust what you hear.

You just might have fun!

Voices of the Earth

A rock can teach you much
more than a person. You just
have to be able to slow down
and listen.

-Spring Bay

Scott Little Crow

Walk to the ocean, in the soft sand, in the place of calm blue water and wash your face in the morning sun.

-Dolphin

Voices of the Earth

Take a rinse in the pure, calm waters of life.

-Frog

Scott Little Crow

Freedom comes from within.

-Great Frigate Bird

Voices of the Earth

It is a knowing that there is no "right" way.

-Great Frigate Bird

Scott Little Crow

Enjoy the ride.

-Dragonfly

Believe in yourself. Trust in your intuitive knowing. Trust in your silent knowledge instead of your programming.

-Black Cat

How can you find anything if
you are blinded by doubt?

-Moss (told to Brita)

Glide; go with the wind; hover;
be still, effortless and graceful.

-Great Frigate Bird

See the beauty in all things.

-Thistle

Slow down, listen to your true nature, ignore the noise on the surface, follow your deep desires and let go of all your excuses for not doing it because they are just ways in which you stop yourself.

-Makaleha Stream

Maintain a solid ground and
everything will come to you.
Then discern with what you wish
to engage.

-Butterfly

When you are feeling distracted by the actions of others, either go deeper inside and intensify your focus, or join them in what they are doing.

-Sugi Pine Tree

Scott Little Crow

If neither is an option, go elsewhere.

-Sugi Pine

You are programmed to fear some things so deeply that your reaction is to run from those things before you have time to think about them or observe what it is that you fear.

-Worm

It is automatic. You move first
and sometimes realize later
what you have done.

-Worm

Sometimes you are not aware of it at all.

-Worm

You can learn a lot from the things you fear if you remain present enough to listen, observe and think before you act.

-Worm

Stamp out the reflex... it no longer serves you.

-Worm

Scott Little Crow

Stop complaining and see the beauty.

-Hanalei Valley

It's OK to wallow in the mud for a while. But one day it will be time to get up; and then it's OK to announce it to the world.

-Hippopotamus

Allow yourself to receive.

Enjoy the present moment. Do not allow the plan or goal to subvert the joy of the action in the present moment.

-Ladybug

You can do all the fun things in the world and go to all the pretty places, but without someone to share the joy, your experience is not as full.

I crossed your path freely. I come and go of my own free will. Do not try to hold onto me, but choose how you will interact with me. Will you treat me with love and kindness? Or will you drive me away?

-Owl

Outer doing is a reflection of inner being.

Voices of the Earth

Sometimes in life, even when we think we know what we are doing, we are in the grips of a force that is so much larger than us that we have no choice but to surrender to it.

-Ladybug

Scott Little Crow

Nonetheless, we must act impeccably; we must act as if we know exactly what we are doing and accept each moment as it unfolds.

That force is so powerful that it is foolish to hope to control the outcome of our lives. Our only recourse to free will is the impeccability of our actions.

-Ladybug

Be still, observe, await your moment and then hop in decisively to capture your game. Excess movement is not necessary; watch the ebb and flow, the tide of emotions and interactions, then at the precise moment...act!

-Frog

Scott Little Crow

"Teach me," you ask, and we say, "Listen, listen carefully and tune in." When you ask a question, really listen to the answer.

-Kaupea Spring

Look around before you come
out of your hole.

-Crab

Listen to your spouse. Do not pre-judge based on what you expect to hear – it is not evidence to prove a theory or your opinion.

You can feed neediness forever. It can be a black hole. Take care of yourself and stay on your own path.

-Black Cat

This does not mean that you should abandon compassion. Take time out, do service, feel tenderness and love. Enjoy being of service to others, but do not completely fulfill the needs of another or they will have nothing to do.

-Black Cat

If they know nothing but neediness, they will become bored after the initial high and take you for granted. Lovers and children often play this role.

-Black Cat

Let me fly free, but keep an eye on me. Only help me if I ask... and then do so willingly. Fly free on your own and we can play together. Walk in beauty and I will walk by your side. Stray and I will fly away.

-Moth

Big, strong trees grow from little seeds.

-Redwood Tree

Take one step at a time.
Be still, stay motionless,
observe... then make your move.

-Frog

Even if you have many moves
planned ahead, just make one
at a time.

-Frog

The whole side of the body is grounded by the foot. Having a firm ground to launch from enables flight.

-Pueo

Be aware of focus.

-Pine Tree

Scott Little Crow

Sometimes camouflage is
necessary for survival.

-Inchworm

We don't always have to stand up and announce our presence to the world.

-Inchworm

We are here, still and silent... spider in its web, lizard in the crack of the rock... waiting. We are all here waiting for our opportunity, hidden in the cracks and the shade. Look carefully around you and observe. This is not evil. This is the way of the world.
Life feeds on life.

-Kaupea Spring

A caterpillar moves by crawling. You are a caterpillar now, so embrace the slow and steady progress. One day you will be a butterfly and fly.

-Caterpillar

Don't make it harder than it has to be.

-Pine Tree

Just because it is quick and easy does not prevent it from being profound.

-Pine Tree

Accept the fruits of life as they come to you.

-Avocado Tree

Step in, make a full commitment and receive great blessings... withdraw and receive very little.

-Eagle

Scott Little Crow

Trust yourself first.

See the big picture, use your wings and fly.

-Spotted Eagle Ray

Don't be afraid of shining too brightly. No one will go blind from the light.

-Bear

Sometimes you have to go out
on a limb to get the job done.

-Mouse

Listen! Pay Attention! You can
learn something now. Send out
all of your feelers, poised,
sensing with all your limbs.

-Gecko

Use your direct perception (intuition). Trust it, it is real. There is no need to run to a book or to others for interpretation.

-Moth

Investigate thoroughly until you are completely satisfied... regardless of what anyone else thinks.

-Mouse

Honor yourself and you will
honor others

-Kauluapaoa

The Goddess must be free to spread her wings while keeping her legs closed.

-Makaleha Spring

If you didn't have your own
issues about this, it wouldn't be
a challenge for you.

-Makaleha Stream

Scott Little Crow

It is natural that you will enjoy some people more than others; however, you must love and accept them all as part of the web.

-Hikina'akala

If you cannot appreciate this, just picture yourself walking around your city and being the **only** person there. Imagine that you have entered into a time warp and wherever you go, every building, every park, every road, is totally deserted except for you.

-Hikina'akala

Now imagine how lonely it would be if you were the only human in the whole world.

-Hikina'akala

True friendship allows free will
and respects the free will of
your friend.

-Makaleha Stream

Scott Little Crow

It is OK to lean on friends in life.
Look at me; I climb up, and
with their help I reach the light.

-Philodendron

Voices of the Earth

If you are feeling too choked by
people leaning on you, simply
break out in a new direction

-Hau Bush

There is no judgment here, it is just part of the dance.

-Philodendron and Hau together

We need a balance of Air, Fire, Water, Earth and Space in order to flourish.

-Hau

Roots must be broad and spread wide. Not too shallow or you may fall, and not too few and deep or you may break.

-Redwood

Even rocks crumble so that old walls can fall. If you want to recreate spontaneous love, let go of the weight of expectation and enjoy the time we are given to spend together without chaining yourself to notions of how it should be.

Scott Little Crow

We do not have to struggle
against the present in order to
change the future.

It is in the stillness of the moment that eternity drifts.

-Nu'alolo A'ina Valley

Scott Little Crow

Writing or speaking about your love is fine, but it is best to show your love with your actions. Words convey intention, and our actions don't always support our intention.

-Koa Tree

Voices of the Earth

Only fear numbs our hearts.

-Dolphin

Scott Little Crow

Sometimes you have to remember where you came from in order to get out of where you are.

-Dove

If we rely on others to fulfill us, then we become chained by our attachment to their actions and may try to subvert their will. Freedom comes from being fulfilled from within, being fulfilled by the beauty of this world around us.

-Snake

Return to the innocence and the mystery of being.

Jump into the waters of life.

-Tadpole

Receive your nourishment from
the Earth Mother.

-Boynton Canyon

Learn to remain still, calm, grounded and observant as the world moves around you.

-Moth

Don't get swept away by the
tide of emotions.

-Frog

If you are feeling sensitive and have your shell up, it is okay to say, "I am feeling crabby and I don't want to talk about it right now."

-Crab

It is your birthright to fully
express your soul.

The joy and vigor of youth come from the strength with which we bring energy up from the Earth... just like a young tree that has burst forth from seed and become established.

-Redwood

Connect your actions with your reason for being in the world.

Keep your eyes open.

-Bee

Follow the magic. It is your choice: magical or mundane, spiritual or material, vibrant or lifeless.

-Black Hawk

Are you sure that you see me?
Pay attention! Take a closer
look!

-Spider

Scott Little Crow

Maintain a peaceful and harmonious rhythm in your life.

Don't be afraid to get dirty and mess up your hair.

-Monkey

Your time here is limited; don't waste it.

Voices of the Earth

Be Free!!

-Pueo

Keep it simple. The essence of the situation is not overwhelming, but rather, quite small.

-Frog

That frog gave me a look that saw through all my bullshit at once.

-Jim Lamont

We do not need for others to accept accountability for their actions in order to have closure. When we are able to have closure regardless of the feelings of the other participants, it gives us autonomy and the power to forgive.

-Makaleha Stream

Allow little things to go easily.
Let go of little parts of yourself
or else someone may pull
harder and a deeper tear will
occur.

-Redwood

The things we release serve to fertilize the ground around us... just as bark that has crumbled off a tree and turned to dust.

-Redwood

Reach out towards the light.

-Aloe Vera

Keep to your spirit path and
trust your intuition.

-Owl

Flow, flow, flow... wherever you go.

-Pine Tree

Scott Little Crow

When abundance comes, give with the heart.

-Spirit of the Earth Mother

Land where it feels right.
Pick your own place and sit.
People may stare at you, but
that is OK.

Observe them as they come and
go; and learn from them all.

-Butterfly

Having your home on your back
means being comfortable
wherever you are.

-Turtle

If you are too jumpy, it is hard to interact and learn from others.

-Fly

In order to maintain your strength and confidence, do things at your own pace in the order and manner that you see fit.

-Leopard

Be mindful of your energy.
Close yourself off and do not
engage with people who are too
aggressive.

-Sugi Pine

Even though we may be acting lovingly in a situation, the other person may not be able to accept our love at the moment.

-Spirit of the Wind

Not all ways of expressing love
are appropriate in every
situation

-Spirit of the Wind

If a spring stops flowing, the life will leave. Nothing will feed on it anymore, because the flow of life has stopped.

You are the spring. Do not stop flowing. Flow, give forth, rejoice in your life - and accept that others will come around to drink.

-Kaupea Spring

When the time is right, stand up and speak your truth without fear.

-Eagle

Take your time. If you jump too early, you give away your position.   Be present, feel, evaluate. Pause - then act.

-Jaguar

Find your center.

-Jaguar

Once you have found it, face
your challenges from there.

-Jaguar

Fly free now, while you can.
You are alive! Even the
greatest of birds will one day die,
so soar and enjoy your life.

-Pueo

If you allow fear to prevent you
from flying, you will never fly
but you will still die.

-Pueo

There is no price for your healing, no promise you must make to have it.

-Rubber Tree

Remember that we all have our own power to access... even when we think that we are victims.

-Eagle

Unify with your purpose.
Remain whole and connected.

-Eagle

Progress can be swift and direct without being frantic.

-Crow

There is a delicate balance
between the spiritual and
physical world. If we get too
caught up in either, we will lose
our balance.

-Spider

You may abandon boundaries in relation to the spirit world, but boundaries must be maintained in the physical world. An example is when someone approaches too closely or aggressively.

All animals know this.

-Crow & Eagle

Why remain in a place where you are disrespected?

-Leopard

There are many forms of love and many ways to express and share those forms of love. At times, those ways and forms change and we may feel disappointment because the new form does not meet our expectations.

-Spirit of the Wind

Events we consider annoying, inconvenient, or inconsiderate may actually be serving a purpose that only becomes known to us later.

-Tortoise

Scott Little Crow

If we are clear about our intentions, it empowers our will. Then we are less easily swayed from our course.

-Makaleha Stream

Remain focused on your project although it may not reap rewards in the short term.

-Ant

Scott Little Crow

Take a good look around before
you jump off or fly away.

-Egret

Follow the light, joy and bliss...
this is the path of the one heart.

-Quartz Crystal

Be adaptable, use your voice to project yourself when necessary, but also be silent and hide when appropriate.

-Kai-ō-té (Coyote)

Allow opportunities to come to you.

-Spider

Do not limit yourself. Express yourself in multiple ways simultaneously.

-Poke Root

There is no need to box yourself
into preconceived modes of
expression or ways of being.

-Poke Root

God **is** nature... **all** of it!

-Cannabis Flower

Sometimes a major shift in our life can be as simple as just letting go.

-Koke'e

Only you are responsible for
your own happiness.

Glide silently like the night and do your work regardless of if anyone is watching.

-Owl

Open like a flower to things and people that nourish you. Be soft and beautiful; blossom to them. Encourage them and lead them into your softness when they are kind to you, but be thorny and sharp if they threaten to harm you or to go where they do not belong.

-Thistle

Be aware of where you put your feet. Watch your step. Territory that seems open and barren may be inhabited by someone who is very protective of it so tread mindfully.

-Poison Ivy

Scott Little Crow

New growth can still come from an old trunk, especially if you cut away the dead branches.

-Beach Almond Tree

Voices of the Earth

Until we see the beauty within us, we cannot see the beauty of the world around us.

What is fragmented can become whole.

-Koa Tree

Love and enjoy the present
moment and all the people in
your life right now because you
never know how much longer
they will be in your life.

-Mi Ling (My Siamese Cat)

Don't forget to run and play
(especially with your mate).

-Mouse

Voices of the Earth

One of the greatest joys of having a physical body is the ability to sense, play and interact directly in the physical world.

-Golden Eagle

When you are whole, you smile.

-Koa Tree

How can you see the beauty if
you are always talking?

-Hanakapiai Falls

Erosion is a natural force. It is the way of the web. Having a strong foundation will give you greater strength and longevity, but eventually all things will fall.

-Grovesnor Arch

Just because you have been a certain way in the past does not mean that you must continue to be that way today. If you want to change, change. It **is** that simple.

You can sprout up in a new direction from the same old foundation.

-Beach Almond Tree

It doesn't matter if anyone else
gets it; just follow your heart.

-Shama Bird

Show your colors vibrantly.
Express yourself with joy no
matter what your surroundings
or circumstance.

-St John's Wort

Sometimes you have to stick your neck out to get places in life.

-Snail

Often we don't know that we're trapped. We don't want to see what others are trying to tell us. We resist moving on even when it is obvious to the people around us that it is time.

We just keep banging into the same window thinking that because we can see through to the other side we can get there quickly and directly.

-Dove

There are thorns along with the fruit. Don't become so ambitious for the fruits that you get caught up in the thorns.

-Rose Hips

Transformation happens in its own time, allow it to be.

-Butterfly

Take seeds of doubt and turn them into hope.

-Quartz Crystal

Walk through the fire. Do not be scared. It purifies.

-Pele

People only fear "hell" because they cannot see its purpose.

-Pele

"Hell" is where we are purified by fire. Where we release our past and move on.

-Pele

"Hell" is only hell if we try to go back to where we came from. It is similar to some types of therapy where people get stuck in the process and never emerge again into the world. These people are truly in hell, eternally burning in the fire of their own pain and suffering.

-Pele

It is essential to continue forward, through the darkness and unknown.

-Pele

Soon, we emerge again in
present time; reborn, purified
and made of pure light.

-Pele

If you follow the path of your heart, you will find treasure. Do not deviate because of preconceived notions in your mind.

-Poli'hale

Trust your inner voice.

-Seed

Scott Little Crow

Keep a strong foundation. Root deeply and support yourself. Bringing strength from the earth through a strong foundation gives you strength.

-Grovesnor Arch

Always choose the path of most power.

-Golden Eagle

Saying things to be
accommodating is not powerful.

-Golden Eagle

Some will love you and some
will judge you.

-Butterfly

A lack of power leads to an inability to speak the truth and induces us to run away from our challenges.

-Golden Eagle

Be who you are in the world fearlessly. Share your ideas and your light with your community.

-Redwood

We are the final authority... God is within us all.

You never have to betray
yourself again.

-Hikina'akala

Life is full of experiences. The field is varied and full.

Practice discernment.

Pick discriminately amongst the many grains of sand.

Slow down, relax....
be joyful.

Take only what you wish to experience.

-Grasshopper

Voices of the Earth

Follow Your Heart!

-Pueo

Scott Little Crow

It is no longer acceptable to sell our light for money.

The new paradigm is that we must create wealth and receive abundance in a manner that simultaneously generates light and nurtures love.

-Quartz Crystal

Directing your inner light to do work that creates more light rejuvenates and replenishes the spirit.

-Fire Spirit

Money contains the spirit of the work done to earn it and the spirit in which it is given.

-Spirit of the Earth Mother

The simplest beliefs that are deep within us can lie hidden for years directing the course of our lives... and then one day we wake up, become aware and decide to change.

-Koke'e

We are given abundance because of our ability to shine light in the world. Continue to shine light and you will be provided for. Do not shine your light and you may obtain money but not happiness.

-Poli'ahu

If you love someone, you must
treat them with love.

Scott Little Crow

There is a big difference between owning something and using it.

Accept abundance as it crosses
your path.

-Poli'hale

Scott Little Crow

It is your life... your choice.

-Eagle

BLOOM!

-Passion Flower